THE SHOSHONI

ALDEN R. CARTER

THE SHOSHONI

Franklin Watts   New York   London   Toronto   Sydney   A First Book   1989

First Paperback Edition 1991

Map by Joe LeMonnier
Cover photograph courtesy of Scott Klette/N.S.M.
Photographs courtesy of: David Muench: p. 11; Utah State Historical
Society: pp. 16, 23 (bottom & left), 28, 33, 37, 58; M. Wheat, *Survival
Arts of the Primitive Piautes*, The University of Nevada Press: p. 17;
Philbrook Art Center: p. 18; Smithsonian, Department of Anthropology:
pp. 20, 25, 34 (top); Idaho Historical Society: pp. 23 (right), 56; Photo
Researchers: pp. 24 and 41 (Tom McHugh/Museum of the American Indian);
Museum of the American Indian, Heye Foundation: pp. 25, 27;
Gilcrease Institute: pp. 29, 55; American Museum of Natural History:
pp. 34 (bottom), 43; Buffalo Bill Historical Center: p. 46; National Collection
of Fine Arts, Washington, D.C.: p. 49; Granger Collection: pp. 51, 53
(both); Paul Conklin: p. 59.

Library of Congress Cataloging-in-Publication Data
Carter, Alden R.
The Shoshonis / by Alden R. Carter.
p.   cm.—(A First book)
Bibliography: p.
Includes index.
Summary: Introduces the lifestyle and culture of the Shoshoni
Indians of the Great Basin.
ISBN 0-531-10753-1 (lib.)/ISBN 0-531-15605-2 (pbk.)
1. Shoshoni Indians—Social life and customs—Juvenile literature.   2. Indians
of North America—Great Basin—Social life and customs—Juvenile literature.
[1. Shoshoni Indians—Social life and customs.   2. Indians of North America—
Great Basin—Social life and customs.]   I. Title.   II. Series.
E99.S4C37   1989
979'.00497—dc19   89-31102   CIP   AC

CONTENTS

For the Kroeplins

*Many thanks to all who
helped with* The Shoshoni,
*particularly the staff of
the Marshfield Public Library;
my editor, Iris Rosoff;
my mother, Hilda Carter Fletcher;
and my friends
Don Beyer, Dean Markwardt,
and Georgette Frazer.
As always, my wife, Carol,
deserves much of the credit.*

THE SHOSHONI

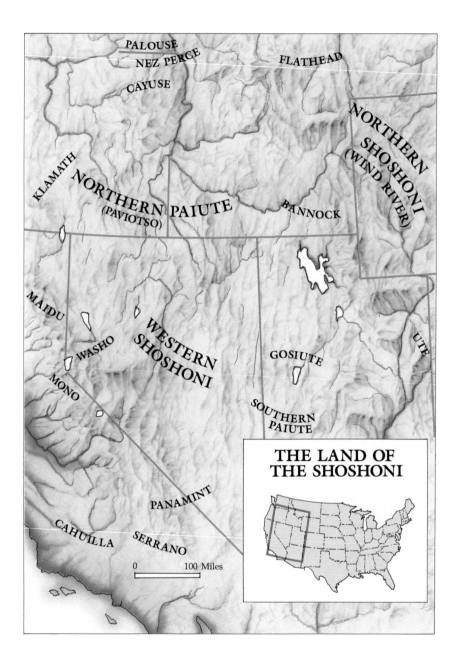

PALOUSE

NEZ PERCE

FLATHEAD

CAYUSE

NORTHERN SHOSHONI (WIND RIVER)

KLAMATH

NORTHERN PAIUTE (PAVIOTSO)

BANNOCK

MAIDU

WESTERN SHOSHONI

WASHO

GOSIUTE

UTE

MONO

SOUTHERN PAIUTE

PANAMINT

CAHUILLA

SERRANO

0   100 Miles

THE LAND OF THE SHOSHONI

PEOPLE OF THE GREAT BASIN

The rain clouds sweep across California from the Pacific to stack up against the high peaks of the Sierra Nevadas. Trapped by the mountains, the clouds open, and rain turns the land to the west a rich green. Only a few clouds slip through to water the huge, barren region beyond the mountains. This is the Great Basin, one of the most rugged areas in North America. Perhaps only the Arctic is less friendly to human beings. Yet, for ten thousand years, hardy, determined peoples have won a slim living in this harsh land. This is the land of the Shoshoni.

The Great Basin stretches from the Sierra Nevadas on the west to the Wasatch Mountains on the east, and from the Snake River and Columbia Plateau on the north and northwest to the Colorado River and Mohave Desert on the south and southwest. Its 200,000 square miles (520,000 sq km) include the eastern edge of California, nearly all of Nevada, the western half of Utah, and the southeastern corners of Idaho and Oregon.

The Basin is not bowl-shaped, but a land of dry valleys and low mountain ranges running from north to south. The Basin received its name because almost none of the rain that falls within its borders finds a way to the oceans. Instead, the Basin's streams and small rivers flow into landlocked lakes and marshes. At the end of the last ice age, about ten thousand years ago, melting glaciers left huge lakes in the Basin. The hot Basin sun dried up most of these lakes. The Great Salt Lake of Utah is the only large lake remaining today. Like the Great Salt Lake, most of the lakes in the Basin are salty.

The Basin is a desert. Most areas receive less than 10 inches (25.4 cm) of rainfall a year and many areas get only 5 (12.7 cm). Temperatures in the summer soar far above 100°F (38°C). In the winter, temperatures plunge to 0°F (−18°C) and below. Yet, a surprising number of plants and animals thrive under those harsh conditions.

The climate has not varied greatly since the first Indians entered the Basin near the end of the last ice

BENEATH SNOW-CAPPED MOUNTAINS,
THE PARCHED SOIL OF THE GREAT BASIN

age. These Paleo-Indians (*paleo* means early) were hunters like their ancestors, who had crossed from Siberia to Alaska fifteen to forty thousand years before. But the great animals of the ice age were rapidly disappearing, and the Basin's first dwellers learned to live by foraging—wandering in search of small animals and edible plants. It took great skill to survive in the desert, and the desert peoples wasted nothing that could be used.

For thousands of years, life changed little. The desert foragers roamed their vast land looking for food. The desert never gave enough for them to settle in one place for long. Most of the year, they moved in small groups of a few families, carrying only the handful of tools needed for hunting and gathering. In the fall, widely scattered groups met to harvest pine nuts and to hunt rabbits. They ground the nuts into flour, feasted on rabbit meat, and made robes of rabbit skin to protect them in the coming winter, the only season when they needed much clothing. These weeks under the autumn sun were a time of celebration—a time for the families to talk, sing, dance, play, court, and renew friendships.

Around A.D. 400, some of the desert people in the eastern Basin adopted a more settled way of life. Members of the Fremont Culture built small villages and grew a few crops, but foraging remained the normal way of life throughout most of the Basin.

About a thousand years ago, a new people began spreading across the Basin from the southwest. They called themselves Numa—the People—and they were the ancestors of the modern Shoshoni. Short-legged and dark-skinned, they spoke a language called Numic, a branch of the Uto-Aztecan family of languages. Over the next few hundred years, they expanded northward, following the foraging ways of the earlier desert peoples.

We do not know what became of the peoples who lived in the Basin before the Numa. The Fremont culture collapsed, perhaps because of a drought, and all trace of the other early desert peoples also disappeared. Perhaps they left the Basin, or perhaps the Numa absorbed them through marriage. By 1300, the only non-Numic-speaking people remaining in the Basin were the Washo, a small, peaceable tribe living on the eastern slope of the Sierra Nevadas.

In fanning out across the Basin, the Numa split into three branches: the Northern Paiute, the Shoshoni, and the Southern Paiute. Each branch developed its own language over the years, but they remained close in most other ways. Paiute and Shoshoni traded with each other and sometimes cooperated in a hunt or a harvest. Young people sometimes chose mates from a neighboring group. So closely were the three branches related in origin, lifestyles, and customs that some scientists group them under the single name Shoshoneans.

Life in the Great Basin continued much as it had since the arrival of the first Paleo-Indians. Year in and year out, small family groups moved with the seasons in the never-ending search for food. Young people courted, married, raised children, grew old, and took the ghost road to the land of the dead. They left behind children and grandchildren who would follow the same cycles. Life in the desert was hard but peaceful and not without pleasure. The sun rose and set on each generation as it had on all the hundreds that had gone before.

LIVING IN THE DESERT

The Shoshoni spent the snowy winter months in mountain valleys or near the foot of mesas, the flat-topped mountains common in the Basin. They chose campsites near springs and sources of firewood. From two to ten families camped together, but even the largest camps rarely had more than fifty people.

In some areas, the Shoshoni used caves for shelter, but usually they built huts from materials they could find nearby. A typical hut was shaped like a cone without a point. A family began by gathering stones to form a ring or by digging a hole wide enough for the base. Poles were set up and woven together with twine made from reeds or bark. This framework was covered with whatever material lay at hand: brush, willows, bark, grass, or earth.

ABOVE: A TEMPORARY SHOSHONI SHELTER.
FACING: RABBIT SKIN ROBES WERE ESSENTIAL
TO THE PEOPLES OF THE GREAT BASIN. SINCE
DEER, ANTELOPE, AND MOUNTAIN SHEEP WERE
IN SHORT SUPPLY, RABBITS WERE THE ONLY
CERTAIN SOURCE OF WARM CLOTHING.

About six people could take shelter inside. A fire burned at the center, its smoke rising through the hole at the top. Food saved through the seasons of roaming fed the people through the long months of winter. Rabbit-fur robes kept the Shoshoni warm. Sometimes, men climbed onto the mountains on snowshoes to hunt bobcats, winter birds, or mountain sheep. But winter hunting was hard, and more often than not, the men returned with little to show but tired muscles and aching stomachs.

The families spent most days repairing fish and rabbit nets, chipping flint arrowheads and knives, carving bows, feathering arrows, and making the other equipment needed for foraging. Women were wonderful basket-makers. The Shoshoni knew how to make pottery, but they preferred basketry. Baskets were light, sturdy, and far better suited to the Shoshoni's wandering life than heavy, fragile pots. Shoshoni women used slender willow branches to make caps, bowls, cups, ladles, trays, and a large variety of gathering, carrying, and cooking baskets.

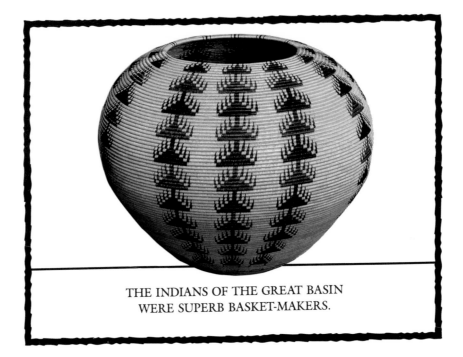

THE INDIANS OF THE GREAT BASIN
WERE SUPERB BASKET-MAKERS.

Evenings were a special time. When the fire burned low and the family snuggled together for warmth, the storytelling began. Parents and grandparents told the stories passed down from generation to generation. Wide-eyed children heard how Wolf had created the earth and how his brother Coyote had made the Shoshoni. A colorful world of gods, men, animals, spirits, and demons came alive in the shadows cast on the walls by the sagebrush fire.

By late winter, food supplies often became a worry. All but the youngest remembered times of hunger in years past. If spring came late, the Shoshoni might starve. Meals were reduced in size, and many an adult went to bed hungry so that children might sleep with full stomachs.

As the days grew longer and the weather warmed, the families began spending more time out of doors. When the ground squirrels awoke from their winter's sleep, the adults breathed easier. Spring had arrived. Men and boys hunted the quick little animals, using smoke or water to force them from their holes into the open where they could be clubbed with a stick or shot with a bow and arrow.

The winter camps broke up when the cattails began to poke through the marshes. Women braved the raw air and the icy water to harvest the first fresh vegetables of the season. The crisp white stems provided

SOME OF THE HUNTING EQUIPMENT
USED BY THE SHOSHONI

needed vitamins and a welcome change in diet after the months of eating pine-nut cakes and dried meat.

Spring was a time of plenty. April brought great flights of ducks and geese from the south. The men strung nets across marshes and ponds and placed decoys made of reeds and feathers nearby to lure the birds from the sky. When a flight landed, the men leaped from their hiding places to startle the birds into the nets. Other birds fell to blunt arrows shot with long-practiced aim. On shore, the women cleaned and cooked the birds. Meanwhile, young boys and girls searched the tall grass for egg-filled nests. Curlews and killdeer provided targets for youngsters learning to use the bow and arrow.

Spawning fish swam upstream in May. Even the Basin's small streams often provided great numbers of salmon, shiners, bullheads, suckers, and trout. The Shoshoni speared, clubbed, and netted the fish, then smoked them over fires. Fish and pine-nut flour made a nutritious soup. The cooking was done by dropping heated rocks into watertight baskets. Squaw cabbage, watercress, clover, and thistles rounded out the meal.

By late spring, the marshes and streams were shrinking fast under the hot desert sun. The Shoshoni roamed in groups of two or three related families, searching for whatever food nature provided. An average family had six or seven people: two or three children, their parents, an aged grandparent, and an unmarried aunt or uncle. A foraging group rarely numbered more than twenty people.

A foraging group covered hundreds of miles in a summer. Some familiar spots produced food one year, almost nothing the next. The families made camps as close to water as possible. The Shoshoni knew every possible source of water in the desert and were highly skilled at finding their way by landmarks, the sun, and the stars. When they had to cross waterless regions, they filled special baskets with water. The tightly woven baskets were sealed with pine pitch to make them waterproof. Water was precious. Without it, a person died quickly in the blazing heat.

The Shoshoni needed little clothing in the summer. Men wore a loincloth of antelope or deer hide, and women an apron of hide or woven sagebrush fiber. Both sexes usually walked barefoot, protecting their feet with pine pitch. Only when the going was particularly rough were the Shoshoni likely to wear sandals made of woven rushes or bark. To protect their skin from the sun and insects, the Shoshoni used a paste made of clay. Babies were wrapped in rabbit skins or antelope hide and carried on frames of willow or chokeberry wood.

Every available hand was needed for foraging. As soon as children could walk, they joined in the search

IN THE SUMMER, THE
SHOSHONI WORE LITTLE
CLOTHING, BUT AT OTHER
TIMES, SOME OF THEM
DRESSED LIKE THIS.

SHOSHONI WOMEN
CARRIED THEIR BABIES
ON THEIR BACKS.

THIS SCENE OF A BISON HUNT
IS PAINTED ON ELK SKIN.

for food. The families hunted lizards, snakes, insects, birds, rodents, and cottontail rabbits. The hunting took great skill and endless patience. A Shoshoni might crouch motionless for hours, waiting for the opportunity to hook a lizard from a hole or to spring a snare on a cottontail. Only dogs and coyotes were not eaten—dogs because of their usefulness as hunting companions and sentries, and coyotes because of the Shoshoni's respect for Coyote, the powerful supernatural being.

More important than hunting was the gathering of wild grasses, roots, and berries. During a summer, the Shoshoni might harvest over a hundred different kinds of wild plants. Both men and women joined in the search, but women were usually the experts. The importance of their skill gave women equal standing with men in Shoshoni society.

GATHERING SEEDS, BERRIES, AND ROOTS WAS AN IMPORTANT PART OF THE SHOSHONI LIFE.

When a promising area was found, the families camped for a few days. Since they would soon be moving on, they made only rough shelters. A tripod of sticks covered on two sides with rush mats or brush provided cover from the sun and wind for two or three people. Rain was rare, and in a downpour the families often had to move quickly to higher ground. A hard rain could turn dry creek beds into raging rivers and wide plains into lakes. Rain was always welcome but often dangerous.

In midsummer, wild grasses made up much of the Shoshoni diet. The seeds from grasses such as pickleweed and rice grass were gathered by shaking or beating the heads of the plants so that the seeds fell into small gathering baskets. These baskets were emptied into larger carrying baskets worn on the back. In camp, the seeds were heated on trays with rocks hot from a fire. The heat opened the husks and freed the edible kernels inside. Gentle tossing kept the trays and seeds from burning and scattered the light husks over the edges—a process called winnowing. The kernels were ground into flour on a stone slab called a metate with a loaf-shaped stone called a mano.

After the Shoshoni gathered a crop of grass seed, they often set fire to the field. Burning cleared away the inedible stalks without hurting the roots, and the ash would fertilize a new crop. The families might also

A SHOSHONI WOMAN WINNOWING

scatter some of their gathered seed on the field. The Shoshoni knew that Indians elsewhere grew corn and other crops, but the desert made farming difficult. Harvesting many different types of wild plants was far safer than depending on two or three crops that might fail and leave the people to starve.

SEEDS BEING GROUND ON A STONE METATE WITH A STONE MANO.

As the summer wore on, different plants ripened. The Shoshoni moved from place to place, harvesting seeds, berries, and roots. Every seven years or so, great clouds of grasshoppers darkened the skies, and the Shoshoni harvested the insects. They dug a hole 10 to 12 feet (3 to 4 m) wide and 4 or 5 feet (about 1.5 m)

AN ENCAMPMENT OF HORSE-OWNING SHOSHONI.
THE TIPIS SHOW THE INFLUENCE OF PLAINS TRIBES.

deep, then formed a wide circle and drove the grass-hoppers inward until the pit filled with millions upon millions of them. Grasshoppers could be dried in the sun for later use, cooked in soup or porridge, or roasted on sticks over a fire.

When the Shoshoni gathered more food than they could carry, they left the extra in grass-lined holes covered with stones and brush to protect it from animals. Late in the fall, the people would return to these caches and carry the food to their winter campsites.

As the days grew shorter, the Shoshoni began looking forward to the annual pine-nut harvest. The piñon pines grew in the mountains, 2,000 to 3,000 feet (600 to 900 m) above the Basin floor. Every four or five years, a stand of the pines produced a rich crop of sweet, oily nuts about the size of olive pits. As fall approached, the families sent out scouts to look for a stand ripening in that particular year. Successful scouts spread the word among the foraging groups of the area.

The families gathered, setting up camp near friends and relatives perhaps not seen in a year. Late into the night, there was talk and laughter around the fires. News was exchanged. The yampa plants had been plentiful near this mesa, the buffalo berries on the far side of that stream bed. The scouts had seen unusual numbers of antelope and, for the first time in years, there might be enough for a big hunt. An old man or woman had died and taken the ghost trail to the land of the dead. Some young men and women had come of age and were seeking mates. Several children had been born of matches made at last year's harvest.

Most of the families of an area were related by blood or marriage. A band had no chief and little formal organization, although some older men and women were particularly respected for their wisdom and experience. A new family drifting into a gathering was quickly accepted; anyone was welcome to work and share in the harvest. Bands usually took the name of a plant or animal common in their area; for example, prairie-dog-eaters or sunflower-seed-eaters. Bands rarely competed or fought with neighboring bands. Friendship was the rule, and it was not uncommon for people to marry into another band or to join a different band for a change of company and scenery.

Much of the first day of the harvest was devoted to dancing and prayer. On the second day, the work began in earnest. Boys climbed the trees to shake the cones from the branches. Men used long poles to knock cones from the tops of the trees. Girls and women gathered the fallen cones and carried them to camp in large baskets. Older women knocked the nuts from the cones with wooden beaters, baked and winnowed the nuts, and then ground the kernels into flour.

For two or three weeks, the harvest continued. Rich pine-nut soups and cakes made bellies full and spirits high. The Shoshoni found time for games when the day's work was done. They shot arrows at targets, threw sticks at rolling hoops, tossed dice, and played a ball game similar to soccer. Feats of juggling fascinated children and adults alike. Everyone spent hours playing or watching a guessing game, called the hand game. It was rather like a complicated form of "Button, button, who's got the button?" Players on one side passed decorated pairs of bones back and forth, while singing, swaying, making jokes, and using sleight of hand to confuse the other side. Score was kept with wooden sticks.

After supper and before the dancing began, the band gathered to talk and tell stories. An elder of the band might make a speech, encouraging the people to be kind to one another and to honor the spirits of the land. A skilled storyteller might entertain the people, his story reminding them of Shoshoni traditions. These gatherings were also a time to settle disputes. If two families had argued, all the other adults tried to patch up matters. If a misdeed needed punishment, the group discussed the penalty. Usually, a few sharp words were enough to shame a wrongdoer into better behavior.

Almost every night the families sang and danced under the leadership of the best dancer. The Shoshoni

THE POPULAR INDIAN GAME
KNOWN AS THE HAND GAME

SHOSHONI LOVED DANCING, AND OFTEN DANCED LATE INTO THE NIGHT. DRUMS WERE AN IMPORTANT PART OF SHOSHONI MUSIC AND DANCING.

had only drums, rattles, rasps, and four-holed elderberry flutes—their only instrument that could play a melody—but they had music in their hearts. Late into the nights, they sang of the beauty of their land and of the joy in their simple, brave life.

During the harvest celebration, young men and women looked for mates. Families sometimes arranged marriages, but more often young people chose for themselves. There was little or no ceremony to a Shoshoni wedding. Once a couple began occupying the same shelter, everyone considered them married. For a few seasons, the new couple remained with the husband's parents, or more often the wife's, before setting out to forage on their own. Sometimes two brothers married two sisters to form a foraging group. The hard desert life made it necessary for every adult to have a helpmate. If a woman lost her husband, she often married his brother. A man who lost his wife often married her sister. If the band had more young women than men, a man might take two wives, usually sisters, and if there were too many men, a woman might take two husbands, usually brothers.

By early October the harvest was over. In the rare years when antelope were numerous, the band prepared to make a drive. Hunting the fast and easily spooked antelope was very difficult with a bow and arrow. For a successful hunt, the band needed the services of an antelope shaman, or medicine man, who had special skills to charm the beautiful animals.

It was the shaman's job to lure the antelope into a narrow place—a box canyon or a disguised corral—where the hunters could shoot them easily. The shaman cast his spell by singing, shaking a rattle, and waving a stick, feather, or piece of fur. Curious, the antelope would come to investigate. Moving backward slowly and carefully, the shaman would lead them into the trap.

As prized as the antelope were for their meat and soft hides, jackrabbits were far more important to the Shoshoni. In November, the band set out to hunt the jackrabbits under the leadership of a skilled hunter known as the "rabbit boss." He directed the placing of nets across the mouth of a valley. The nets were woven of twine made from milkweed bark, dogbane, or Indian hemp. Two feet (0.6 m) high and hundreds of yards (meters) long, the nets were family treasures passed down from generation to generation.

The rabbit boss divided the band into hunters and beaters. While the hunters waited at the nets, the beaters started from the far end of the valley on a smoke signal from the boss. Shouting and beating the brush, they drove the jacks toward the nets. The object of the nets was not to catch the rabbits but to cut off their escape. The nets were delicate, and the hunters

HUNTING ANTELOPE WITH A BOW AND
ARROW WAS NOT AN EASY TASK.

tried to kill as many of the jacks as possible while the rabbits milled about trying to find a way out of the trap. Jacks that burst through the nets or became entangled caused damage that would take long hours to repair.

Everyone took a hand in cleaning the rabbits and preparing a feast. In the days following the hunt, the women made fur robes of the rabbit skins. Starting at the outside edge, they cut the skin in a spiral toward the center, producing a continuous strip of fur about an inch (2.3 cm) wide and perhaps 15 feet (5 m) long. The strips were stretched between poles about 6 feet (2 m) apart. Under the heat of the sun, the edges curled inward until the strips became furry ropes. More ropes were added and then all were tied together in perhaps a dozen places to produce the robe. A child's robe took around forty rabbit skins, an adult's as many as a hundred. Quivers, muffs, and infant blankets were also made of rabbit fur.

As the air grew chilly, the band broke up to search for winter campsites and to retrieve caches of food left on the Basin floor. The golden fall was over; the time of cold, hardship, and even starvation lay ahead. Yet, spring would come again, then summer, and finally another fall when the band would meet again to celebrate the joy of being Shoshoni.

THE LIFE OF THE SPIRIT

The Shoshoni's world was alive with spirits. Every bush, bird, animal, rock, lake, and mountain had a spirit. Wandering ghosts made the whirlwinds that spun across the desert floor. Angry giants sent rocks tumbling down mountainsides, and evil dwarfs caused sickness with invisible arrows. But most spirits were kindly and, if treated with respect, would help the Shoshoni.

The Shoshoni wandered their land, always aware of the spirit world about them. When they found roots or wild grasses, they made an offering to the spirit of the place. Hunters said prayers of thanks when an animal gave its life so that families might eat. The

Shoshoni religion had no priests, secret societies, or fancy ceremonies. Every Shoshoni lived in daily contact with the spirits, following the simple rule that where respect was given, good fortune was returned.

At night, children learned about the spirit world from their parents and grandparents. The Shoshoni, like all Indian tribes, never developed a written language. All stories had to be passed down through telling and retelling. Some stories taught children how to behave. Others tried to explain the origins of the Shoshoni or the workings of the desert world. Many of the tales were very funny and sent the family to bed laughing.

Above the simple shelters of the Shoshoni, the clear desert sky blazed with stars. Like people all over the world, the Shoshoni found figures of men, women, and animals in the constellations. They gave the brightest stars and the roving planets names and stories. The Milky Way held a special place in the heavens. This was the ghost trail, the road that departed souls followed to the land of the dead.

Coyote strode through the stories of the Shoshoni, shifting shapes as often as shadows thrown by a campfire—now a man, now an animal, sometimes brave, wise, and kind, sometimes cowardly, foolish, and selfish. He played tricks on the other supernatural

THIS PAINTING ON MUSLIN DEPICTS THE SUN DANCE.
THE SHOSHONI LIVED IN DAILY CONTACT WITH THE
SPIRITS THAT INHABITED THEIR WORLD.

beings—Wolf, Eagle, Rabbit, Skunk, Chipmunk—but was often doubly tricked in return.

According to most stories, Coyote was the mischievous younger brother of Wolf, who created the world. Coyote made the Indians, then invented pine nuts and freed the animals from Wolf's corral so that the Indians would have food to eat. He also gave them fire, showed them how to weave baskets and make tools, and taught them to pray. (The word for *pray* in Shoshoni translates as *Coyote-talk*.)

The Shoshoni also believed in a higher being than Coyote and the other supernatural beings with animal names. Appe, the creator of the universe, was visible as the sun, which gave life and light to the world. (We do not know if the Numa brought this idea to the Basin or if it developed later). However, Appe was distant, and most prayers and offerings were made to the spirits who lived in the world and could do the Shoshoni immediate harm or good.

Spirits appeared to some people in dreams and visions, giving them special powers and responsibilities. A man—or occasionally a woman—so blessed became a shaman. A shaman might have the power to charm animals, cast magic, or cure the sick.

Life in the desert was never easy. Sickness and death visited the camps frequently. The Shoshoni often went hungry or lacked important vitamins in their diet.

MANY DIFFERENT ITEMS WERE USED IN
VARIOUS DANCES AND CEREMONIES. THESE
OBJECTS WERE USED IN THE WOLF DANCE.
THEY INCLUDE: (A) APRON, (B) FEATHER BUSTLE,
(C) EAGLE FEATHER FAN, AND (D) DANCE WAND.

Hunters in the mountains risked bone-breaking falls. Foragers on the desert floor had to watch for poisonous snakes.

The Indians of the Great Basin used an amazing number of plants as medicines. One scientist counted some three hundred, including fifty-two for colds and forty-eight for stomachaches. When everyday remedies failed, the shaman was summoned. He brought his spells, magic powders to throw in the fire, and totems—items of special power, often oddly shaped stones or small figures made of leather, feathers, and sticks.

If a patient suffered from sharp pains, an invisible arrow or other sharp object was blamed. The shaman would suck, blow, or brush at the spot where he thought it had entered. Around the fire, family members added their voices to his chants. If the patient lay unconscious, it was thought that his or her soul had wandered away or been stolen. The shaman would fall into a trance, sending his own spirit in search of the soul that might, at that moment, be treading the ghost trail toward the land of the dead.

Most female shamans were midwives, women skilled in helping mothers through childbirth. The midwife chanted spells and gave painkilling herbs while the mother was in labor. The husband waited nervously, hoping he had remembered to obey all the taboos—rules that had to be followed if the mother and child were to survive. For example, a couple expecting a child would never make a corded rope out of fear that the baby would be strangled in the womb by the umbilical cord. Despite all that the midwife could do, many mothers and babies died.

When death took a Shoshoni, the family usually burned the hut and the dead person's possessions with the body. The tools a hunter had used in life would help him on his journey to the land of the dead. The burning of his body protected the living, since the spirits of the dead were greatly feared. The family group mourned the loss of one of its own, but life had to go on. Soon the place of death was left behind, lost in the desert haze as the soul of the departed disappeared forever into the spirit world.

In their wanderings, the Shoshoni took special note of certain places. At a spot where a Shoshoni hunter had good luck, he might pause to paint or carve an animal figure or other symbols on a rock. The Shoshoni also painted their bodies. Both men and women wore earrings and necklaces made of bones and shells. The skilled hands of women produced some of the most beautifully decorated basketry in the West.

But the greatest art of the Shoshoni was their way of life. In one of the most hostile regions on the continent, they used a thousand skills to feed themselves, to raise their children, and to live in harmony with nature and the unseen spirit world beyond.

Every fall, when they gathered to harvest the pine nuts, the Shoshoni danced the round dance. Singing to the rhythm of the drums, they moved round a tall pole reaching toward the sun. The spirit of Appe, the life-giver, shone down on his people, who danced in a circle without beginning or end—a wheel like the revolving seasons, like the cycle of birth, life, and death forever turning beneath the desert sun.

THE SHOSHONI PRAIRIE BY THE FAMOUS
ARTIST FREDERIC REMINGTON

THE BROKEN CIRCLE

The fall of 1521, according to the white man's calendar, might have been any other year for the Shoshoni gathering for the pine-nut harvest. But events far to the south would change the Shoshoni way of life forever. After nearly two years of fighting, Hernán Cortés, a Spanish soldier of fortune, was on the brink of destroying the great Aztec Indian empire in Mexico. The white man's conquest of North America had begun.

The Shoshoni who danced the round dance that year would never see a white man. Isolated in their rugged land, some Shoshoni would not see one of that hairy, pale-skinned race for another three hundred years. But the influence of the white man would seep into the Great Basin long before the first white explorer arrived.

The Spanish conquest spread north from Mexico. The Spanish brought guns, iron tools, military organization, a new religion, and a new way of travel—the horse. The horse produced a revolution in the Indian way of life over much of the American West. A mounted Indian could move faster over a much wider area than his footsore ancestors. He could swoop down on his enemies, then escape with the speed of the wind. Most important, he could follow the great buffalo herds far better than any Indian afoot.

The Indians of the Southwest became the first mounted tribes. They traded horses with their northern neighbors. By the early 1700s, horse ownership was spreading rapidly. The horse changed the way of life of nearly every tribe. Indians turned from foraging to hunting, and from living in small areas to roaming over vast distances. They traveled in larger groups and became more organized. Tribes such as the Sioux and Cheyenne became rich and powerful buffalo-hunting nations on the Great Plains east of the Rocky Mountains.

Shoshoneans on the fringes of the Great Basin adopted the mounted way of life. Bands that had crossed the mountains into Wyoming became the Eastern, or Wind River, Shoshoni. A large number of

WHILE MOST SHOSHONI IN THE GREAT BASIN FOUND
HORSES AN IMPOSSIBLE LUXURY, THEIR COMANCHE
COUSINS USED HORSES TO BECOME THE GREATEST
WARRIORS AND HUNTERS OF THE SOUTHERN PLAINS.

Eastern Shoshoni moved south, becoming the Comanche, the most feared warriors of the southern plains.
In southern Idaho, Northern Paiute and neighboring
Shoshoni joined to become the Bannock Shoshoni. In
southwestern Utah, a branch of the Southern Paiute
split away to become the Ute. These groups soon became more like Plains Indians than their kin in the
Basin.

Within the Basin, most Shoshoneans did not accept the horse. Horses ate the wild grasses so important in the diet of the desert peoples. Buffalo were few in the Basin and most desert hunting and gathering was done more easily on foot. When the Basin Shoshoni caught or traded for a horse, they usually ate it.

The ownership of horses by surrounding peoples hurt the Basin Shoshoni. The best grasses and hunting areas along the borders of the Basin were soon closed to them by their newly rich and powerful neighbors. Utes raided the poor camps of the Basin Shoshoni. Captured women and children were sold as slaves to the Spanish and the Indian tribes of the Southwest. The Shoshoni who still followed the age-old ways retreated deeper into the Basin.

Spanish explorers and missionaries were the first white men to enter the Basin. Father Silvestre Escalante traveled through the southern Basin in 1776. Other explorers followed, but none of them stayed long.

In the 1820s, fur traders and trappers began to take an interest in the region. The fur trade brought more of the white man's inventions into the Basin. In earlier generations, the Basin's Indians had traded food and hides among themselves. Tribes outside the Basin had traded buffalo skins, pottery, and obsidian (a hard rock ideal for stone arrowheads and tools) for the unequaled work of Shoshoni basket-makers. Shells from

FUR TRAPPERS BROUGHT TRADE GOODS AND THE
WAYS OF THE WHITE PEOPLE INTO THE BASIN.

the California coast and the great rivers of the Northwest were greatly prized for necklaces and earrings by
the Basin Indians. Shells had also served as money in
at least part of the Basin. But the white trader offered
new riches: copper cooking pots, brightly colored cloth
and beads, and iron arrowheads, knives, and hatchets.

When the market for furs declined in the early
1840s, some fur traders turned to leading the first wagon
trains across the Basin to California. In 1843–44, the

great explorer John C. Frémont mapped the Basin. A steady stream of wagon trains followed. When gold was discovered in California in 1849, the stream became a flood. Hundreds of wagon trains crossed the Basin on trails miles wide. The livestock ate Shoshoni grasses and muddied water holes. The whites looked down on the nearly naked desert people, calling them "digger Indians," after their practice of digging for roots with long, pointed sticks. Indians living near the two main trails began adopting the mounted way of life. They followed the wagon trains, taking anything they could use from the mountains of goods the whites threw away to lighten their wagons. Angry over the damage to their land, the Indians soon began raiding the trains themselves for horses and food.

Meanwhile, the eastern Basin was filling with Mormon settlers. The Mormons had come west in search of a place to practice their religion. They settled near the Great Salt Lake in 1847 and soon established ranches, farms, and small towns throughout western Utah. Some Mormons tried to get along with the Shoshoni and Utes of the area, hiring many of the Indians as ranch- and farmhands and teaching them to use modern tools. But misunderstandings and raids by both sides led to fighting, and the Mormons crushed the Shoshoni bands that tried to defend the land they had lived on for centuries.

TOP: A MORMON ENCAMPMENT IN UTAH. DESPITE
EFFORTS AIMED AT A PEACEFUL COEXISTENCE,
THERE WERE CONFLICTS AND TENSION BETWEEN
THE MORMONS AND SHOSHONEANS. BOTTOM:
STREET SCENE IN SALT LAKE CITY, UTAH.

The western Basin was not safe for long. In 1859, silver was discovered in Virginia City, Nevada, bringing a flood of miners from California. Ranchers and townspeople followed. The settlers cut down the piñon pines for fuel and fence posts, built their towns and ranches in the best valleys, and fed their cattle and pigs on the wild grasses and roots. Weakened by hunger, the Indians died by the hundreds from diseases brought by the white man.

For a time, some of the Shoshoni tried to fight back, but they had never been a warlike people. They lacked numbers, guns, and experience. Used to traveling in small foraging groups, they lacked the tribal organization for warfare. The army quickly defeated the few mounted bands that chose to fight. Almost all the Shoshoni without horses sadly but quietly accepted the end of their age-old way of life. In 1863, most of the Indian bands in the Great Basin started signing peace treaties with the U.S. government.

The government failed to live up to many of the promises made in the treaties. Food and other goods arrived late or not at all. Reservations were located on poor land or far from areas familiar to the bands. Some Shoshoni families refused to move and tried for a few more years to continue their old way of life in the lands still unsettled by the white man.

IN TREATIES WITH THE UNITED STATES GOVERNMENT,
THE SHOSHONI AGREED TO MOVE TO RESERVATIONS
IN EXCHANGE FOR REGULAR PAYMENTS OF GOODS
AND MONEY. OFTEN THE GOVERNMENT FAILED TO
KEEP ITS END OF THE BARGAIN.

CONDITIONS ON RESERVATIONS WERE HARD. THE WOMAN
IN THE CENTER IS A PRESBYTERIAN MISSIONARY.

Always hard, the foraging life soon became impossible. Many Shoshoni had to beg white farmers and
ranchers for work and food. Others drifted to the
mining towns, the men taking low-paying jobs and
the women working as maids or doing the laundry for
white families. All too often, the Indians had to pick
through garbage cans to find enough to eat. The once
proud and independent Shoshoni had reached the low
point in their history.

For half a century, the Shoshoni lived on the edge of extinction. The government was slow to provide jobs, health care, and food, but quick to carve away large chunks of treaty land, until some reservations were only a quarter of their original size.

The Shoshoni did not find it easy to band together to fight for their rights. Used to the independence of small family groups, the Shoshoni had to learn to work in larger organizations. In the 1930s, they finally formed their first tribal organizations. Slowly, living conditions began to improve.

Eventually, many whites began to appreciate that the Indians whom white settlers had once despised as "diggers" were actually the masters of desert survival. Few peoples anywhere in the world had lived so long and so successfully in such a rugged land. Scientists came to the Basin to learn from the Shoshoni some of the wisdom that had enabled the Indians to live in harmony with nature and each other.

As times improved, the Shoshoni population recovered. In 1873, the government had estimated the Shoshoni population at about fifty-five hundred. Today, there are around sixteen thousand. About three-quarters live on or near reservations at least part of the year. Including the other Shoshonean tribes and the unrelated Washo, about forty thousand Indians live within or on the borders of the Basin—about double the population in 1873 and around the same number as scientists estimate lived in the Basin before the white man came.

The Shoshoni face many challenges in the late twentieth century. Many Shoshoni individuals now hold highly skilled jobs as teachers, lawyers, doctors, nurses, heavy-equipment operators, and the like. However, a large number of Shoshoni lack full-time work, and average family income is low. Diet, health care, education, and housing need improvement.

ABOUT SIXTEEN THOUSAND SHOSHONI NOW LIVE
ON OR NEAR RESERVATIONS IN THE WEST.

ALTHOUGH MANY CUSTOMS AND TRADITIONS HAVE
BEEN FORGOTTEN BY THE SHOSHONI, THERE IS
A MOVEMENT UNDERWAY TO PRESERVE THE RICH AND
VALUABLE HERITAGE OF THIS PROUD PEOPLE.

Over the years, many of the old customs and skills were forgotten. Today, many Shoshoni living off the reservations can no longer speak the language. Tribal organizations and individuals are working hard to preserve the old customs and to meet the needs of the modern Shoshoni.

Despite all the hardships the Shoshoni have suffered, their spirit remains strong. A Shoshoni ranch hand walking to the corral at dawn may wear a Stetson, work shirt, jeans, and boots, but his stride is as smooth and easy as his ancestors'. His senses effortlessly record every sound and smell of the awakening desert, and his keen eyes watch for the faintest movement on the far mesa turning red in the first light of the new day. He is undefeated—still independent, still proud of his skills, and still in love with this hard, beautiful land.

FOR FURTHER READING

Bierhorst, John, ed. *In the Trail of the Wind*. New York: Farrar, Straus and Giroux, 1971.

Claiborne, Robert. *The First Americans*. New York: Time-Life Books, 1973.

D'Amato, Janet, and Alex D'Amato. *Indian Crafts*. New York: The Lion Press, 1968.

Glass, Paul. *Songs and Stories of the North American Indians*. New York: Grosset & Dunlap, 1968.

Hirschfelder, Arlene. *Happily May I Walk: American Indian and Alaskan Natives Today*. New York: Scribner, 1986.

Hofsinde, Robert (Gray-Wolf). *Indian Sign Language*. New York: Morrow Junior Books, 1956.

Kopper, Philip. *North American Indians Before the Coming of the Europeans*. Washington: Smithsonian Books, 1986.

Maxwell, James A., ed. *America's Fascinating Indian Heritage*. Pleasantville, N.Y.: Reader's Digest, 1978.

Whiteford, Andrew Hunter. *North American Indian Arts*. New York: Golden Press, 1973.

INDEX